Slimy • Scaly • Deadly
Reptiles and Amphibians

LIZARDS

Gareth Stevens
Publishing

Please visit our Web site www.garethstevens.com. For a free color catalog of all our high-quality books, call toll free 1-800-542-2595 or fax 1-877-542-2596.

Library of Congress Cataloging-in-Publication Data
Lizards / Tim Harris, editor.
       p. cm. -- (Slimy, scaly, deadly reptiles and amphibians)
       Includes index.
       ISBN 978-1-4339-3426-1 (library binding) -- ISBN 978-1-4339-3427-8 (pbk.)
       ISBN 978-1-4339-3428-5 (6-pack)
       1. Lizards--Juvenile literature. I. Harris, Tim.
    QL666.L2L594 2010
    597.95--dc22

                                           2009039215

Published in 2010 by
Gareth Stevens Publishing
111 East 14th Street, Suite 349
New York, NY 10003

© 2010 The Brown Reference Group Ltd.

For Gareth Stevens Publishing:
Art Direction: Haley Harasymiw
Editorial Direction: Kerri O'Donnell

For The Brown Reference Group Ltd:
Editorial Director: Lindsey Lowe
Managing Editor: Tim Harris
Children's Publisher: Anne O'Daly
Design Manager: David Poole
Designer: Sarah Williams
Production Director: Alastair Gourlay
Picture Researcher: Clare Newman

Picture Credits:
Front Cover: Shutterstock: Fivespots, Shutterstock: Maxim Petrichuk.

JI Unlimited: 8b, 9t, 14b, 23t, 23b; Shutterstock: Alexandro Axon 25t, John Bell 14t, 21t, Alex James Bramwell 28t, Lucian Coman, Lucian 20b, Steve Cukrov 6b, Dan70 25b, Sebastian Duda 4, Brian Dunne 11t, Fivespots TP, Andrzej Gibasiewicz 28b, Kato Inowe 18t, IW1975 18b, Falk Kienas 20t, Jill Lang 11b, Steve Lovegrove 24t, Timothy Craig Lubcke 16b, Robyn Mackenzie 26t, Merryl McNaughton 10, Claus Mikosch 5b, Phil Morley 19t, Hiroyuki Saita 27b, Steffen Foerster photography 6t, 13b, T. W. 24b, Robert A. Van Het Hof 5t, Judy Worley 9b.

All Illustrations © The Brown Reference Group plc.

Publisher's note to educators and parents: Our editors have carefully reviewed the Web sites that appear on p. 31 to ensure that they are suitable for students. Many Web sites change frequently, however, and we cannot guarantee that a site's future contents will continue to meet our high standards of quality and educational value. Be advised that students should be closely supervised whenever they access the Internet.

Manufactured in the United States of America
1 2 3 4 5 6 7 8 9 12 11 10

CPSIA compliance information: Batch #BRW0102GS: For further information contact Gareth Stevens, New York, New York at 1-800-542-2595.

Contents

A piece of old skin hangs off a lizard's neck.

Why do lizards shed their skin?

Lizards have skin that is covered in hard scales. The scales are made from keratin, the same stuff as in fingernails and hair. The scales make the skin waterproof, so lizards can live in dry places without drying out too much. However, there is a problem: the skin does not grow with the rest of the lizard, and the scales do not stretch much. So as the lizard grows, its skin gets tighter. Eventually, the outer skin splits off from the body, showing fresh skin underneath.

Do you know...?

A lizard's skin is shed in several scraps. Because of the animal's body shape, the skin breaks into pieces. Snakes do not have legs, so they shed their skin in a single tube (right). A snake's new skin is brightly colored, but it soon fades.

How does a basilisk run on water?

Basilisks can run about 5 feet (1.5 m) per second.

Do you know...?

Diving lizards are small iguanas that live in the flooded forests of the Amazon. The lizards live in the trees, but if they are attacked, they leap into the water below.

Basilisks are lizards that live close to water. They have an unusual way of escaping from a predator—they dash across the surface of the water. A basilisk is able to do this because each of its long toes has a fringe of scales around it. The scales give the foot a large surface area, which spreads the basilisk's weight across the water's surface. As long as the lizard keeps running, it won't sink.

How do horned lizards scare off enemies?

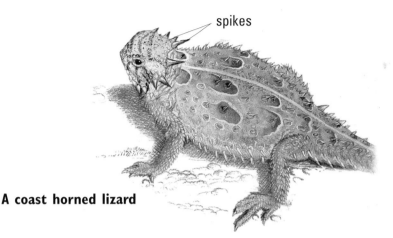

spikes

A coast horned lizard

Horned lizards are plump lizards that live in the deserts of North America. They have a rather disturbing defense technique. When a horned lizard meets an enemy, it takes some deep breaths to puff itself up so it looks as big and fierce as possible. It does not stop there—the lizard then squirts the attacker with a stream of blood from its eyes! That is usually enough to stop a predator in its tracks.

Do you know...?

Horned lizards form a group called the *Phrynosoma*. This name means "toad body" because the lizards have a plump body like a toad's. In parts of Mexico and the United States, the lizards are called horned toads.

Which is the only lizard that lives in the sea?

A marine iguana

Some lizards live along the shoreline, but only one spends much of its time in the sea: the marine iguana. It lives on the Galápagos Islands in the Pacific Ocean. Marine iguanas spend much of their time in the ocean. They eat seaweed that grows underwater and must dive down to graze on it. The lizards have wide, rough lips that are good at scraping slippery seaweed from the rocks. When they are not feeding, the iguanas sunbathe to dry off and warm themselves.

Do you know...?

Marine iguanas are black. That color helps them absorb the heat from sunlight and warm up after a chilly swim. However, some male marine iguanas look a little different: they develop striking red and green blotches during the summer breeding season.

A Gila monster eats a desert rodent headfirst.

Why is a Gila monster such a monster?

The Gila monster earns the name "monster" for its striking appearance. It is a brightly colored hunting lizard. Gila monsters and Mexican beaded lizards are the only lizards to kill prey using venom (a poison) in the saliva. The venom gets into their victims' blood when the lizards bite them. The venom works slowly, and a lizard has to hold prey in its powerful jaws as it waits for the victim to die.

Do you know...?

The Gila monster and its neighbor, the Mexican beaded lizard, have unique scales. No other reptile has the same rounded scales that form shiny bumps on the back. Unlike in other reptiles, the scales do not overlap.

Why do water monitors bury eggs in termite mounds?

Do you know...?

Laying eggs is a matter of life and death for some kinds of chameleons. Most of these lizards dig a trench to bury their eggs. Female Mediterranean chameleons lay a total of thirty eggs, which can weigh up to half the lizard's body weight. After devoting so much energy to producing such a large quantity of eggs, many of the females die after just one breeding season.

Water monitors are large lizards. The adults have few enemies, but their eggs are at risk of being eaten by other animals. Water monitors enlist the help of stinging termites to keep hunters away. The female digs a nest in the termite mound, and the eggs develop in the safety of the mound. When the young monitors hatch, they eat some termites for their first meal!

These water monitors live in Africa.

How does an anole attract mates?

Anoles are close relatives of iguanas, and most live in the forests of South America. Their green and brown colors help keep them safely hidden among the trees. However, keeping out of sight is

A male anole shows off his dewlap.

not so useful during the breeding season. At this time of year, the male anoles want to get noticed by females. Anoles do this by extending a flap of skin under the chin called a dewlap. Once extended, this reveals bright pink, red, or yellow skin that is normally hidden from view. Different species have different colors on their dewlaps.

Do you know...?

Green anoles are unusual because they live farther north than other anoles—in the southern United States. It can get cold there, and when it does the pale green lizards turn dark brown. Even the pink dewlap changes color.

Why does the fat-tailed gecko have a fat tail?

A fat-tailed gecko

Fat-tailed geckos live in dry grasslands. They hunt at night for insects before burrowing into sand or leaves to spend the day out of sight. During droughts, the geckos find it hard to catch enough food. They have to survive for days on a store of food inside their fat tail. The store is kept well stocked when there is plenty of food around. During hard times, the tail becomes thin as the food is used up.

Do you know...?

A six-lined grass lizard's tail is four times as long as its body! That allows it to move like a snake when it needs to escape from predators. It holds its short legs against its body and wriggles along the ground.

Why do barking geckos bark each evening?

A barking gecko

It is usually easier to hear a barking gecko than to see one. These small lizards live in the deserts of southern Africa. They use their wide, spadelike feet to dig tunnels in the soft sand. They stay underground during the day to avoid the intense heat. At sunset, male barking geckos come to the entrance of their burrows. Despite their name, the geckos produce a series of loud "tock" noises to attract mates. However, the calls also attract dangerous enemies, such as owls. If a gecko is attacked, it runs back into the burrow, where most hunters cannot follow.

Do you know...?

Barking geckos can hide from most predators in their complex burrows. However, small snakes follow them underground. The geckos still have an escape route. They flee down a dead end that actually leads to a hidden exit, then burst out into the open and run away.

Why do some geckos have vertical pupils?

This large gecko's pupils are narrow slits.

Most geckos are active at night, or nocturnal, and their eyes are very good at seeing in the dark. When it is dark, an eye's pupil opens wide to let in as much light as possible. Like many nocturnal animals, geckos have pupils that can spread very wide to gather as much light as possible when it is dark. In strong light, the pupils become narrow slits, which protect the sensitive inside of the eye.

Do you know...?

A chameleon finds insects to eat by scanning the surrounding leaves and branches. Its eyes are on the sides of its head, and each eye can move by itself. That means the lizard can look in two directions at once.

Why do web-footed geckos have webbed feet?

A web-footed gecko

You might think that a lizard with webbed feet would live in water. However, the web-footed gecko lives in the Namib Desert, one of the driest places in Africa. This little lizard searches for insects in the sand. Walking on loose sand is tiring for most animals because their feet sink into the surface, and it takes a lot of effort to pull them out again. Web-footed geckos do not have this problem. Their webbed feet work like snowshoes, spreading the lizards' weight so they never sink.

Where does a sandfish swim?

Despite its name, a sandfish is not a fish but a type of lizard called a skink. Like most skinks, a sandfish has a thick, rounded body, a powerful tail, and short legs. It is a skink that lives in the deserts of West Asia. Being active in the day, the lizard is at risk of being attacked by predators such as hawks or jackals. When danger approaches, the sandfish gets away by "swimming" into the loose sand.

Once in the sand, the skink steers using its shovel-shaped snout. It points the snout down to swim deeper, and angles it upward to get back to the surface.

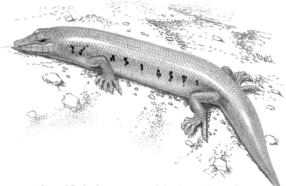

Sandfish have speckled scales that help them stay hidden on the sand.

Do you know...?

Many lizards are excellent swimmers. They use their tails to power themselves forward. Water monitors are large lizards that swim along African rivers hunting for fish and crabs. Out of the water, these lizards dig into crocodiles' nests and eat the giant reptiles' eggs.

Do all lizards have a father?

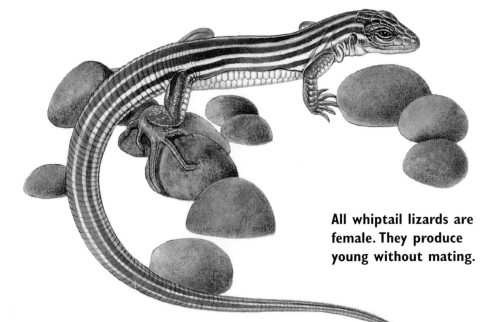

All whiptail lizards are female. They produce young without mating.

It is usual for reptiles to be either male or female. To produce young, a male and female mate with each other. However, a few kinds of lizards can reproduce without mating. The females lay eggs without the help of a male. The eggs all grow into female lizards. The new lizards can also lay eggs without needing a mate. Each lizard has just a mother—there is no such thing as a father.

Do you know...?

Mating is a system that mixes the genes (inherited bits of information) of the mom and dad. That produces young with unique sets of genes. Making young without mating is called asexual reproduction. There is no mixing of genes, so the young have the same genes as their mothers. They are clones. Producing clones helps animals increase in number very quickly.

What do lizards see with their third eye?

It is sometimes possible to see a clear, gray scale on the top of a young lizard's head. This is the window for the third eye. The third eye does not see things, but it can detect light and dark. In some cases it can sense heat, too. If the eye detects a shadow (or heat) passing over its head, it will crouch down or run away because it may mean danger is near.

An iguana senses light through its head.

eardrum

Do you know...?

Lizards do not have ears sticking out of their heads, but they are still able to hear. Sound waves are picked up by an eardrum on the side of the head. The eardrum can be seen in some species (left), but it is usually covered in scales.

What is a bearded dragon's beard made from?

Bearded dragons are lizards that live in Australia. They are covered in rows of spiky scales that provide defense against snakes. Bearded dragons have a bone sticking out of the base of the tongue. When danger is near, the lizard points the bone down. That pulls the loose skin around the throat into a spiky, scary-looking beard.

A bearded dragon

Do you know...?

Garden lizards are sometimes called bloodsuckers. The lizards only eat insects, so where does the name come from? During the mating season, a male's throat and chest turn blood-red. That color attracts mates.

Is a slowworm really a lizard?

Slowworms live across Europe. They are often found under flat stones.

A slowworm's name suggests it is a worm. However, anyone who has seen a slowworm might think it is a snake. Slowworms have no legs and are the size of a large night crawler, but they have scales like a reptile. And a reptile without legs is a snake, right? Well, it is not that simple. Slowworms are lizards that live by burrowing through soil looking for food. They have evolved (changed over time) to live without legs.

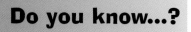

Do you know...?

There are several other lizards that have evolved to live without legs. The black-headed scaly foot makes the most of looking like a snake. It is colored to look like poisonous snakes such as young cobras (below).

A gecko cleans its eye.

Why do geckos lick their eyes?

When we blink our eyelids, we wipe dust off the surface of our eyes. Gecko eyelids are fused shut over the eyes. That creates a protective window over the eyes. Geckos can still see because the eyelids are see-through. But dust builds up on the windows, so geckos have to give them a wash every now and then—with a quick lick of the tongue.

Do you know...?

Some species of geckos do have movable eyelids. Most live in Africa and southern Asia and include the leopard gecko (right). Eyelid geckos live a bit differently than other species. They spend most of the time on the ground and do not have toe pads for climbing.

What is a frilled lizard's neck frill for?

A frilled lizard displays his frill.

The frilled lizard lives in the the dry forests of northern Australia. Frilled lizards are most often seen clinging to a tree trunk as they bask in the sun. A close look shows that the animal's neck and upper back are cloaked in a frill of skin. The frill hides the shape of the animal and helps its brown scales blend in with the tree bark. But the frill is not just for camouflage. If the lizard is scared, it raises the frill into a startling collar and chases its attacker.

Do you know...?

The blue-tongued skink is another Australian lizard with an unusual way of scaring off attackers. When this tough lizard feels threatened, it pokes out its wide blue tongue and shows off the bright pink insides of its mouth. These colors scare predators into thinking that the skink is more dangerous than it is.

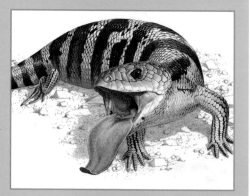

Why does a lizard lose its tail?

Most lizards rely on camouflage to hide from predators. If a hungry hunter does see them, however, lizards have another line of defense. As the lizard runs for its life, a swift attacker might grab its tail. That is not enough to catch the prey, though, because the captured tail falls off! That usually confuses the predator, especially since the detached tail continues to wriggle. The tail buys the lizard enough time to escape. Soon it will grow another tail, although the new one is usually shorter.

The five-lined skink has a bright blue tail that distracts attackers.

Do you know...?

Most chameleons are climbers. They creep along branches, clinging on with their feet. Their tail is used to grip as well, like a fifth foot. The tail is prehensile, which means it can wrap around and grasp a branch.

What does a thorny devil drink?

The thorny devil is a mean-looking lizard that lives in the deserts of Australia. Its whole body is covered in thick spikes, which are especially long above the eyes and on the neck. The lizard's

A thorny devil

thornlike defenses make it tough for predators to eat. The spikes have another purpose. A thorny devil never gets to drink liquid water. It gets some of the water it needs from its food, but it also collects water in another way. Tiny drops of dew form on its spikes. This moisture travels along a network of channels between the lizard's scales. The channels carry a supply of water to the corners of the thirsty thorny devil's mouth.

Do you know...?

American horned lizards are not related to thorny devils, but they look similar to the Australian reptiles. Both lizards are sandy yellow, and both are covered in spines. When two unrelated species live in the same way and look the same, they have evolved to live in similar places.

How do chameleons change color?

Chameleons are amazing lizards that can alter the colors and patterns on their skin to blend in with their surroundings. This changeable camouflage helps them to stay out of sight just about anywhere. Chameleons also use colors to show when they are angry. The chameleon's skin contains three types of colored cells. The lizard can expand and contract the different colors to create a color pattern that matches what the lizard sees around it.

Do you know...?

Geckos can also change color, although no other lizard is as good at changing color as the chameleon. A gecko grows paler or darker to blend in with the background and gets paler when it is hot. The masters of color changes are entirely different: cuttlefish (above) can change color very quickly.

A colorful chameleon

How do geckos walk on ceilings?

A gecko's ridged toe pads

Geckos are fantastic climbers. They can climb up smooth glass and have no problems walking upside down on ceilings. Many geckos have rounded pads on the tips of their toes. These pads are not sticky, but they are covered in folds of skin. These folds are each folded many times to make a toe with a huge surface area. It is this large area that enables a lizard's toe to cling to surfaces.

Do you know...?

It is not just geckos that climb around on flat surfaces. There is a whole group of lizards called wall lizards—because they are often seen climbing on walls and rocks. Unlike geckos, wall lizards grip with long, clawed toes.

Why do Jackson's chameleons have horns?

Jackson's chameleons are lizards that live in the mountains of East Africa. The male chameleons have three horns sticking out from the front of their face. Some females have horns, too, but they are usually shorter than those of the males. The males use their horns in fights during the breeding season. Males lock horns to knock each other off a good perch. The male with the longest horns usually wins because his rival cannot get close enough to push his enemy away.

Do you know...?

Jackson's chameleons are more common than other kinds of chameleons, but it is now illegal to take them out of Africa. However, many years ago some were taken to Hawaii as pets. There, they escaped into the wild and their numbers grew. They are now a common sight there.

The Canary Islands are home to some giant lizards.

What are the giant lizards of the Canary Islands?

The Canary Islands are off the coast of North Africa. These islands are home to some unusual wall lizards. Although they are similar to several North African species, there is one big difference: the Canary Island lizards are giants. The largest grow to almost 3 feet (1 m) long. There are several different kinds, and all of them have evolved into big lizards that can eat large amounts of food.

Do you know...?

By 1940, no one had seen an El Hierro giant lizard for so long that scientists believed they had all died. Then, in 1999, a group of 300 lizards was found in a remote area of El Hierro (right), one of the Canary Islands. The giant lizard had been alive all along!

Why does the bushveld lizard get mistaken for a beetle?

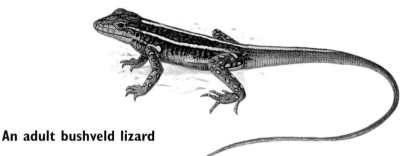

An adult bushveld lizard

The bushveld is the dry area of grass and shrubs that covers much of southern Africa. It is where bushveld lizards live. The adults have a brown and yellow back that helps them hide, but young bushveld lizards look very different. Their tail is a sandy color, but the rest of the body is black with several large white spots. The yellow tail blends in with the ground, making it hard to see. That leaves just the black body in view, which makes the lizard look like a beetle. Young lizards even walk like beetles, keeping their legs stiff and making jerky movements.

Do you know...?

Young bushveld lizards look like oogpister beetles. The name oogpister means "eye squirter." The beetle earns this name because it squirts a nasty acid spray into the eyes of attackers. Small mammals and birds learn to stay away from them. Oogpister beetles only grow to 2 inches (5 cm) long. Once a bushveld lizard grows longer than that, its beetle disguise no longer works well. That is when the lizard takes on its adult colors.

Glossary

bask: to lie in warm sunshine and soak up the Sun's warmth

camouflage: a coloration or body shape that helps an animal blend with—and hide in—its surroundings

desert: an area where very little rain ever falls

evolve: change over a long period of time

iguana: a kind of lizard

nocturnal: active at night

predator: an animal that hunts other animals for food

prehensile tail: a tail that is able to wrap around something and hold on

prey: an animal that is hunted by another animal

scale: a tough, waterproof plate that grows out of the skin of some reptiles

snout: an animal's nose and jaws

species: a group of animals that share features, and can mate and produce young together

venom: a poisonous liquid that a few kinds of lizards (and many snakes) produce. The lizards inject the poison into their victims by biting.

Find Out More

Books about amphibians

Arnosky, Jim. *All About Lizards*. New York: Scholastic, 2004.

Bredeson, Carmen. *Fun Facts About Lizards!* Berkeley Heights, NJ: Enslow Publishers, 2009.

Facklam, Margery. *Lizards Weird and Wonderful*. New York: Little, Brown and Company Young Readers, 2003.

Magellan, Marta. *Those Lively Lizards*. Sarasota, FL: Pineapple Press, Inc., 2008.

Robinson, Fay. *Amazing Lizards*. New York: Cartwheel Books, 1999.

Trueit, Trudi Strain. *Lizards*. New York: Children's Press, 2003.

Useful websites

Frilled Lizards
animals.nationalgeographic.com/animals/reptiles/frilled-lizard.html

Lizards
www.corkscrew.audubon.org/Wildlife/Lizards.html

Types of Lizards
www.factzoo.com/reptiles/types-of-lizards.html

San Diego Zoo's Animal Bytes
www.sandiegozoo.org/animalbytes/t-lizard.html

Index